THE SIMPSONS 2016 ANNUAL

Copyright © 2015
Bongo Entertainment, Inc. All rights reserved.
No part of this book may be used or reproduced in any manner whatsoever
without written permission except in the case of brief quotations
embodied in critical articles and reviews. For information address
Bongo Comics Group
P.O. Box 1963, Santa Monica, CA 90406-1963

Published in the UK by Titan Books, a division of Titan Publishing Group,
144 Southwark St., London SE1 0UP, under license from Bongo Entertainment, Inc.

FIRST EDITION: AUGUST 2015

ISBN 9781783298242

2 4 6 8 10 9 7 5 3 1

Publisher: Matt Groening
Creative Director: Nathan Kane
Managing Editor: Terry Delegeane
Director of Operations: Robert Zaugh
Art Director: Chia-Hsien Jason Ho
Art Director Special Projects: Serban Cristescu
Production Manager: Christopher Ungar
Assistant Art Director: Mike Rote
Assistant Editor: Karen Bates
Colours: Nathan Hamill, Art Villanueva
Administration: Ruth Waytz, Pete Benson
Legal Guardian: Susan A. Grode

PRINTED IN ITALY

SIMPSONS™
COMICS

TITAN BOOKS

SNOW DAD

IAN BOOTHBY
SCRIPT

PHIL ORTIZ
PENCILS

MIKE DECARLO
INKS

ART VILLANUEVA & NATHAN HAMILL
COLORS

KAREN BATES
LETTERS

NATHAN KANE
EDITOR

FIRST RACCOONS AND NOW THIS? SUSAN, WE'RE MOVING!

BART!

THAT'S IT! YOU'RE *GROUNDED* FOR WINTER VACATION! NO LEAVING THE YARD!

WHATEVER.

DAD, WE'RE GOING TO BE LATE FOR THE *HOT CHOCOLATE FESTIVAL*! IF WE DON'T HURRY, WE'LL MISS KRUSTY'S OPENING BIT WHERE HE "ACCIDENTALLY" SCALDS SIDESHOW MEL WITH HOT COCOA!

WHAT? THE FESTIVAL'S *TODAY*?

NOT FOR *YOU*, BOY! FLANDERS WILL BE KEEPING AN EYE ON YOU, AND HE'LL CALL US IF YOU GO ANYWHERE!

I'VE GOT AN *ITCHIN'* TO DO SOME *SNITCHIN'*!

WHY ME?

BECAUSE OF YOUR SINS!

♪ NINETY-NINE MUGS OF HOT CHOCOLATE ON THE WALL, NINETY-NINE MUGS ♪ OF HOT CHOCOLATE...

AND SO...

OH HEY, HOMER, I JUST WANTED TO LET YOU KNOW I'VE GOT NO HARD FEELINGS AND...

PSYCH!

PAF!

PIF!

HMMM...PERHAPS WALKING TO THE SCIENCE FAIR WITH MY NEW *HYDRO-ANIMATOR* WASN'T SUCH A GOOD IDEA ON THIS ICY SIDEWALK!

JUST BE *CAREFUL*, FRINKY...

OH SWEET GLAVIN, I'M MAKING WITH THE FALLING!

KA-POW!

ZAAAP!

SORRY!

NO HARM DONE, YOUNG MAN, EXCEPT TO MY PRIDE... AND MY *COCCYX!* ‡GA-HEY!‡

HEY, IS ANYONE GONNA EAT THIS CARROT?

SWEET BILL NYE'S BOW TIE! MY INVENTION WORKED!

MY SNOWMAN'S ALIVE!

YES, MY HYDRO-ANIMATOR MAKES WATER SENTIENT! YOUR SNOW PERSON NOW HAS A MIND OF HIS OWN!

SO DO I HAVE A NAME OR WHAT?

I'LL CALL YOU SNOWMER!

I HAVE NO IDEA IF THAT'S A GOOD NAME OR NOT, SEEING AS I'VE ONLY BEEN ALIVE FOR TWO MINUTES.

...BUT SURE!

THAT CREATURE IS AN ABOMINATION!

SO I'M AN ABOMINABLE SNOWMAN! BIG DEAL!

HOURS LATER...

I FEEL BAD FOR BART. HE WOULD HAVE LOVED WHEN THE MONKEY ATTACKED KRUSTY WITH THOSE MARSHMALLOWS.

YOU'LL SEE! THIS IS FINALLY GOING TO TEACH BART TO RESPECT ME!

HEY, HOMER! I'VE REPLACED YOU WITH MY NEW DAD, SNOWMER!

GOOD THROW, BOY! I'M PROUD OF YOU!

LATER...

HOMER, YOU'VE BEEN LOOKING OUT THAT WINDOW ALL DAY!

BUT THEY'RE HAVING SO MUCH FUN!

THIS SNOW FORT IS AWESOME!

WAIT'LL YOU SEE THE BASEMENT!

MAYBE IF YOU SPENT MORE TIME WITH BART, HE WOULDN'T TRY TO GET SO MUCH NEGATIVE ATTENTION.

I'VE TRIED!

WELL, TRY AGAIN!

AND SO...

COME ON, CAN'T I JOIN IN YOUR *REINDEER GAMES*?

NO! WE'RE DOING A LIVE READING OF THE *CLASSIC ACTION MOVIE SCREENPLAY*, AND THERE AREN'T ANY PARTS LEFT!

MR. AFFLECK, IT'S YOUR LINE!

GUYS, THIS IS FUN, BUT I REALLY SHOULD BE GETTING BACK TO THE SET OF MY NEW FILM!

SOON...

WHAT TH--?

OH HEY, BART! **SNOWMER JUNIOR** AND I WERE JUST PLAYING HOCKEY!

IT'S NOT FAIR! YOUR BUTT IS BIGGER THAN THE GOAL!

HE'S A GREAT KID!

YOU'VE DONE NOTHING BUT YELL AT ME!

WELL, SNOWMER AND I WERE JUST GOING TO PLAY SOME PINBALL!

IT'S MADE OF ICE AND TOTALLY WORKS! SNOWMER IS **AMAZING!**

HOMER TRIED TO FIX THE TOASTER WITH A FORK ONCE AND WAS IN A COMA FOR TWO WEEKS.

COME WITH ME!

BWA-HA!

14

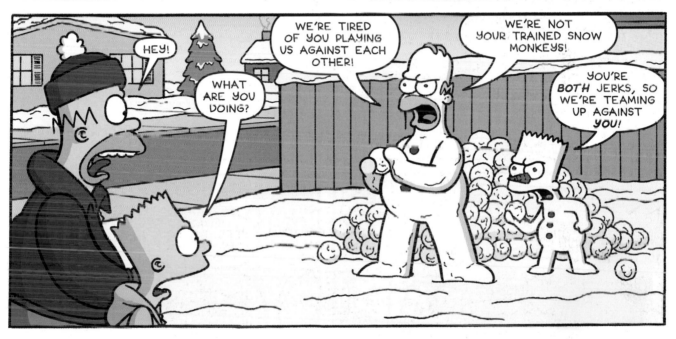

15

HOT CIDER IN THE CITY

HEY, BART, WE'RE GOING CHRISTMAS CAROLING. WHY DON'T YOU COME WITH US?

YEAH, BART! WE'RE GOING A-WASSAILING! DON'T YOU WANT TO WASSAIL?

NAH, I'M ADDING A *NEW TRICK* TO MY *PRANKING REPERTOIRE*.

THROW YOUR VOICE

BUT, BART, WE'RE SINGING "ANGELS WE HAVE HEARD ON HIGH" AND "GOOD KING WENCESLAS"...ALL THE CLASSICS!

WELL, I'M SURE YOU AND *SANTA DORK* WILL HAVE A *GREAT* TIME.

C'MON, MILHOUSE. THERE'LL JUST BE MORE FREE COOKIES FOR US.

FREE? COOKIES?!

HALLELUJAH! IT'S A MIRACLE! I'M SUDDENLY FULL OF THE *CHRISTMAS SPIRIT!* WAIT FOR ME!

YEAH, HE'S FULL OF *SOMETHING* ALL RIGHT...

TONY DIGEROLAMO SCRIPT

JASON HO PENCILS

ANDREW PEPOY INKS

NATHAN KANE COLORS

KAREN BATES LETTERS

BILL MORRISON EDITOR

A FEW CAROLS LATER...

...AND A HAPPY NEW YEAR!

WELL, YOU MIGHT SAY THAT SONG REALLY BLEW ME *AWAY IN A MANAGER!*

AND SINCE THIS IS THE *THIRD TIME* YOU'VE BEEN TO MY DOOR, I'LL GET YOU A DOUBLE HELPING OF FRESHLY BAKED COOKIES!

CAN YOU PUT *TWO* CINNAMON STICKS IN MY HOT APPLE CIDER THIS TIME?

CAN-DOODLY-DO, BART!

MMM...⁞GULP!⁞ ⁞MUNCH!⁞ I CAN'T WAIT TO SEE ⁞GULP!⁞ WHAT FLANDERS MAKES US NEXT! ⁞CRUNCH!⁞

BART, WE'RE SUPPOSED TO BE SPREADING CHRISTMAS CHEER, NOT MOOCHING OFF OF MR. FLANDERS!

I FEEL ⁞CRUNCH—MUNCH!⁞ *CHEERFUL!*

SEE?

LOOK, IT'S THE *THREE WISE DORKS*.

HEY, THIS IS *OUR* CAROLING TURF!

YEAH, NOW GET OUT OF HERE BEFORE I *DECK YOUR HALLS* AND BEAT THE *FA-LA-LA* OUT OF YA!

CAROLERS DON'T HAVE "*TURF*," AND YOU CAN'T CRUSH OUR CHRISTMAS SPIRIT!

♪ LIII-SAAA... ♪ SHUT YOUR ♪ MOUUU-UUUTH. ♪

TRUST US. THEY CAN CRUSH *ANYTHING*.

19

WE'RE TAKIN' OVER YOUR ROUTE, SIMPSON. NOW WHICH HOUSE IS GIVIN' OUT THE CINNAMON STICKS?

NO, BART, DON'T TELL THEM!

LISA, I DON'T THINK I HAVE A CHOICE.

ONE SEASON'S BEATING LATER...

YOU BULLIES AREN'T GOING TO GET AWAY WITH THIS! THIS IS *ANTI-CHRISTMAS!*

HA HA HA HA!

THE ONLY THING YOU'RE GOING TO GET FOR CHRISTMAS IS A LUMP OF COAL IN YOUR STOCKINGS!

OW!

WELL, I GUESS I SHOULD'VE SEEN *THAT* COMING.

OH, BART, NOW WE CAN'T CAROL ANYWHERE. I'M SORRY WE DRAGGED YOU ALONG FOR THIS.

LIS, I'M ABOUT TO GIVE YOU AN EARLY CHRISTMAS PRESENT.

"I DIDN'T SEND THEM TO THE FLANDERS' HOUSE..."

♪ SILVER ♪ BELLS...SILVER BELLS...IT'S ♪ CHRISTMAS ♪ TIME IN THE ♪ CITY... ♪

CHRISTMAS CAROLS FOR *ME*? :SNIFF!: NOBODY'S EVER SUNG ME NUTHIN' BEFORE. I THINK I'M GONNA CRY LIKE A WOMAN HERE.

TING-A-LING...

WATCH ME THROW MY VOICE...

THIS IS TO MAKE UP FOR ALL THE PRANK PHONE CALLS DURING THE YEAR!

WHUH--? THAT WAS *YOU*?!

HEAR THEM RING...

C'MERE, YOU ROTTEN BRATS! ALL YOU'RE GONNA WANT FOR CHRISTMAS IS YOUR *TWO FRONT TEETH* AND A NEW *SPLEEN* WHEN I GET DONE WITH YOU!

AAAAAH!

BART, I THINK YOUR PLAN LACKED THE PROPER CHRISTMAS CHEER.

SO IT'S CHRISTMAS CHEER YOU WANT, EH?

LAST ONE BACK TO FLANDERS' HOUSE IS A ROTTEN ELF!

JOYEUX NOEL!

HERE IS THE COURSE OF ACTION WE SHALL PURSUE: I WILL FORGET ABOUT THIS ACCIDENT, BUT YOU WILL OWE ME *A FAVOR*. IT COULD BE SMALL, YET IT WILL MOST LIKELY BE BIG.

YOU MEAN, LIKE PICKING YOU UP FROM THE AIRPORT? BECAUSE I'M NOT THE BEST DRIVER.

SPRINGFIELD NUCLEAR PLANT

IN FACT, THAT FAVOR WILL BE REDEEMABLE *IMMEDIATELY*.

AT THE LEGITIMATE BUSINESSMAN'S CLUB...

AHH. THE PROVERBIAL *GANG* IS ALL HERE.

HOMER? HOW DID YOU GET ROPED INTO THIS?

SHHH! DON'T USE MY NAME. I WANT TO KEEP MY IDENTITY A SECRET.

COMPLETELY AGREE! *OH YEAH!*

GENTLEMEN. FOR DIFFERING REASONS, YOU ARE ALL FIRMLY IN MY DEBT. AND I HAVE DECIDED TO CALL IN ALL THESE FAVORS AT ONCE.

TO ASSEMBLE A *TEAM*.

THERE IS A RIVAL MAFIOSO IN TOWN, **DON HENLEY**. HE STOLE SOMETHING QUITE IMPORTANT TO ME, AND WE ARE GOING TO RECOVER SAID ITEM.

TONIGHT IS HIS ANNUAL CHRISTMAS PARTY. USING YOUR **PARTICULAR SET OF SKILLS**, YOU WILL BREAK INTO THE PARTY AND RETRIEVE SAID OBJECT.

DO THIS, AND YOUR DEBT IS PAID.

OTHERWISE...

CRACKK!

YOU'LL CRACK OUR KNUCKLES MALICIOUSLY?

OUTSIDE DON HENLEY'S MANSION...

ACCORDING TO FAT TONY, THE BRIEFCASE IS IN A **SECRET ROOM** OFF THE MAIN HALLWAY. WE CAN ENTER **HERE** THROUGH THE DOGGIE DOOR.

I'VE SECURED FOUR SUITS FROM THE CATERING STAFF SO WE CAN BLEND IN. WE GRAB THE KEY AND MAKE IT TO THE VAULT. ANY QUESTIONS?

YO, **TEACHER MAN**... WHAT DID FAT TONY, LIKE, OFFER TO MAKE **YOU** WORK FOR THE MOB?

HE HAD SOMETHING THAT I NEEDED. **BADLY.**

SOON...

AHH. THE SOUND OF FRANK SINATRA SINGING "LET IT SNOW." IS THERE ANYTHING MORE FESTIVE?

DID YOU SEE THE HAPPY LITTLE ELVES SPECIAL TONIGHT? THEY DID THIS ONE DANCE NUMBER THAT, SWEARTAGOD, IT HAD ME LAUGHIN' LIKE A *JAMOKE!*

COME ON, MAN! DON'T *SPOIL* IT FOR ME!

EXCUSE ME? DID THE WAIT STAFF JUST INSULT MY GUEST?

SO, TRAY MONKEY, YOU GONNA APOLOGIZE FOR YOUR VERBAL SLIGHT?

UHH...

THIS LOOKS LIKE A JOB FOR DUFFMAN...

THE
RADIOACTIVE
MAN
CHRISTMAS SPECIAL!

MAX DAVISON
SCRIPT

JACOB CHABOT
PENCILS & INKS

ART VILLANUEVA
COLORS

KAREN BATES
LETTERS

NATHAN KANE
EDITOR

A PAST-HIS-PRIME *DIRK RICHTER* DONNED THE RED AND GOLD COSTUME FOR THE FIRST TIME IN YEARS!

EVEN BUDDY HODGES REPRISED HIS *FALLOUT BOY* ROLE, ALTHOUGH HE WAS FAST APPROACHING MIDDLE AGE.

LEGEND SAYS THAT THE STORY REVOLVES AROUND THE *SUPERIOR SQUAD'S* ANNUAL CHRISTMAS PARTY AND IS PEPPERED WITH CELEBRITY CAMEOS.

A YOUNG *RAINIER WOLFCASTLE* EVEN HAS A SMALL ROLE, ALTHOUGH HE WAS CREDITED AS "RAINIER STRONG."

THE PRODUCERS, HOWEVER, COULD NOT SECURE THE RIGHTS TO *CAPTAIN SQUID,* SO THEY INVENTED A LAME KNOCKOFF TO STAND IN FOR THE FAN FAVORITE CHARACTER.

THE SPECIAL WAS SUCH AN UTTER *DISASTER* THAT THOSE ASSOCIATED WITH IT HAVE CHOSEN TO PRETEND THAT IT NEVER HAPPENED.

MUCH LIKE THE "*LOST*" FINALE.

RUMOR HAS IT THAT THE MORTY MANN ESTATE HUNTED DOWN EVERY LAST COPY AND *INCINERATED* THEM.

BUT THANKS TO MY *BULLSEYE-ESQUE PRECISION* IN EBAY SNIPING, I WON THAT AUCTION AT THE LAST POSSIBLE SECOND!

NOW I CAN WATCH THIS FABLED FLOP FOR MYSELF! HOW BAD COULD IT POSSIBLY BE? THE MIND BOGGLES!

CLICK!

"THE RADIOACTIVE MAN HOLIDAY SPECIAL" WAS RECORDED BEFORE A LIVE STUDIO AUDIENCE.

SOUNDS GREAT, BROADWAY JOE! HEY, TEAM...LET'S TAKE OUR HOLIDAY PICTURE! ARE YOU READY, MR. PHOTOGRAPHER?

OH, YES! OF COURSE!

ALL RIGHT, HEROES. SMILE AND SAY...

ZZAAP!

FREEZE!

WHAT IN THE WORLD?

⸖GASP!⸖ DR. CRAB?!

THAT IS CORRECT, LURE LASS! THEY SAY THAT A PARTY HASN'T STARTED UNTIL SOMEONE *CRASHES* IT!

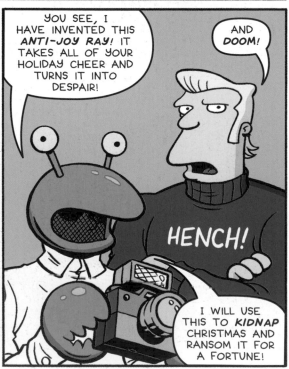

YOU SEE, I HAVE INVENTED THIS *ANTI-JOY RAY!* IT TAKES ALL OF YOUR HOLIDAY CHEER AND TURNS IT INTO DESPAIR!

AND *DOOM!*

HENCH!

I WILL USE THIS TO *KIDNAP* CHRISTMAS AND RANSOM IT FOR A FORTUNE!

WE SHALL *SEE* ABOUT THAT!

ALAKAZAM ALKA-SELTZER!

W-WHAT? WHY AREN'T MY SPELLS WORKING?

BWA-HA-HA! WITHOUT YOUR LOVE OF CHRISTMAS, YOUR POWERS WILL NOT WORK!

THAT SOUNDS SO CRAZY, IT *MUST* BE TRUE!

NOW, TO TEST THE EFFICACY OF THE RAY GUN. WOULD YOU LIKE A *GIFT*, RADIOACTIVE MAN?

NO THANKS. I'M FINE.

SUCCESS!

AND NOW LET US MOVE THIS PARTY TO A MORE *APPROPRIATE* LOCATION...

WELCOME TO MY LAIR, SUPERIOR SQUAD. MAKE YOURSELVES COMFY. AS YOU CAN SEE, I HAVE SOME *COMPANY* FOR YOU.

HENCH!

OY! I AM *SCHVITZING* IN THIS SUIT!

IT'S *SANTA CLAUS!* SO *THAT'S* WHY HE DIDN'T WRITE BACK TO ME!

...

WHAT DID I JUST WATCH?

THAT WAS *TERRIBLE!* AWFUL! IT WAS, WITHOUT A DOUBT, THE ABSOLUTE...

BEST. HOLIDAY SPECIAL. *EVER!*

IT IS SO SPECTACULARLY AWFUL, IT MAKES THE *"EWOK CHRISTMAS SPECIAL"* LOOK LIKE *CITIZEN KANE!*

I CAN MOCK IT FOR DAYS ON END! JUST THINKING ABOUT MY FUTURE JIBES AND CAUSTIC COMMENTS HAS ME POSITIVELY GIDDY! WINTER HAS COME, AND I AM EDDARD *SNARK!*

HUZZAH! A NEW ANDROID'S DUNGEON HOLIDAY TRADITION IS BORN!

RADIOACTIVE MAN STUDIO EDIT COPY NOT FOR RESALE

NOW TO TOAST UP A CASE OF GINGERBREAD POP-TARTS!™ AND WATCH IT AGAIN!

AND TO ALL A GOOD NIGHT!

TONY DIGEROLAMO SCRIPT   **JASON HO** PENCILS & INKS   **CHRIS UNGAR** COLORS   **KAREN BATES** LETTERS   **BILL MORRISON** EDITOR

NOOOOO!

WAAAAAAH!

JEBEDIAH SPRINGFIELD DAY

AND SO I, HEREBY...ER, UH... COMMEMORATE OUR TOWN FOUNDER ON THIS DAY...

A NOBLE SPIRIT EMBIGGENS THE SMALLEST MAN

MAYOR

MMMPHFL... HMMMBL!

OH MY GAWD! THAT *HUGE SNOWBALL* IS...ER, UH...COMING RIGHT AT US!

JEBEDIAH SPRINGFIELD DAY

A COLD DAY IN SPRINGFIELD

PAUL KUPPERBERG
SCRIPT

REX LINDSEY
PENCILS

DAN DAVIS
INKS

ART VILLANUEVA
COLORS

KAREN BATES
LETTERS

NATHAN KANE
EDITOR

MAN, THAT'S ONE *DEEP* SNOWDRIFT!

MUST... FIND...CHEESY PUFFS!

THAT'S NOT A DRIFT. IT SNOWED ALMOST TWENTY FEET LAST NIGHT!

TWENTY FEET?!

YES. THE NEWS SAID WE WERE IN A LOCAL ZONE OF *EXTREME CLIMATE CHANGE* BECAUSE OF A PROBLEM AT THE NUCLEAR PLANT!

HMMM...

MAYBE *THAT'S* WHAT THAT *WARNING LIGHT* WAS FOR!

NUCLEAR WINTER ALERT

AW, MAN! WE'RE *TRAPPED* INSIDE THE HOUSE? THIS SUCKS!

IT'LL BE *FUN!* I'VE GOT A WHOLE LIST OF CHORES FOR *EVERYBODY!*

D'OH!

50

...THAT'S MY LAST OFFER BEFORE I TAKE THIS DEAL TO *SPEED-E-MART*, APU!

VERY WELL, YOUNG SIMPSON. YOU HAVE ME OVER A BARREL... SEVERAL, IN FACT, ALL FILLED WITH FOOD OF DUBIOUS INGREDIENTS.

I WILL SUPPLY GROCERIES AT WILDLY INFLATED PRICES, WHICH YOU WILL THEN DELIVER.

THANK VISHNU I OVER ORDERED ON COLD WAR ERA EMERGENCY RATIONS!

AND SO...

OKAY, DUDES, THANKS FOR COMING ON BOARD. NELSON, YOU'RE TUNNELING TO MOE'S. DOLPH, YOU'RE GOING TO THE RETIREMENT CASTLE.

REMEMBER...YOU ALL GET TO KEEP TEN PERCENT OF THE TOLLS YOU COLLECT ON ANY TUNNEL YOU DIG. NOW, LET'S GET DIGGING!

UH...YOU GUYS SURE YOU DON'T WANT *SHOVELS*?

NAW. SHOVELS'D ONLY SLOW US DOWN!

POW!

PUNCH!

SLUG!

52

WE'RE **COMMANDEERING** THESE TUNNELS, BOY! NOW RUN ALONG!

THAT'S NOT FAIR!

TO MOE'S

TO CARMEL CORN WAREHOUSE

TO CITY HALL

SURE IT IS. WE CALLED *DIBS* IN THE EVENT OF CIVIC EMERGENCY!

LATER, AT THE SIMPSON HOUSE...

WE MAY HAVE LOST THE TUNNELS, BUT THERE'S STILL A *WAR* TO BE WON!

WE DON'T STAND A *CHANCE* AGAINST THEIR SUPERIOR SHOVEL POWER, BART!

TRUE, BUT THEIR SHOVELS ARE ONLY GOOD IN *SNOW!*

MILHOUSE, GATHER EVERYONE AND TAKE THE MONEY WE MADE TO *COSTINGTON'S* TO BUY SUPPLIES. I'LL MEET UP WITH YOU AFTER I RUN A *LITTLE ERRAND!*

SOON...

EXIT

WITH THE TOWN SNOWED IN, THE POWER PLANT'S PROBABLY RUNNING ON A *SKELETON CREW*.

...SO I TELL MR. BURNS THAT IF HE'S NOT PAYING ME, I'M NOT WORKING FOR *FREE* JUST BECAUSE I'M SNOWED IN!

WISH *I'D* THOUGHT OF THAT!

HOMER'S WORKSTATION IS JUST AROUND THE CORNER...

IF THE POWER PLANT *STARTED* ALL THIS SNOW, MAYBE IT CAN *END* IT!

OKAY, HERE WE GO. NOW, IF I CAN JUST REMEMBER WHAT I READ IN THAT *OPERATOR'S MANUAL* HOMER LEAVES IN THE BATHROOM.

ENGAGE THE *RELEASE LIMITS*... OVERRIDE *PRESETS*... VENTS TO THE *MAXIMUM OPEN* POSITION...

LET'S SEE CHIEF WIGGUM DIG HIS WAY OUT OF THIS!

NOW TO RENDEZVOUS WITH THE GANG...AND WAIT FOR THE INEVITABLE!

HEY, WHO WAS THAT?

I DUNNO. MAYBE BURNS IS BRINGING IN PYGMY *SCAB WORKERS*.

LATER, BACK IN THE TUNNELS...

IT SURE IS *WARM*, CONSIDERING WE'RE SURROUNDED BY ALL THIS SNOW.

THAT'S JUST THE SNOW'S INSULATING QUALITIES TRAPPING OUR BODY HEAT, LOU.

TOLL 5.00
TOLL $5.00

ARE YOU *SURE*, CHIEF? DON'T YOU THINK IT'S GETTING KINDA *STUFFY*?

NAH, WE'RE JUST *EVOLVING*. OUR BODIES ARE ADAPTING TO LIVING IN THIS FROZEN UNDERWORLD!

TOLL $5.00

THE END

...A RECORD-SETTING **30 INCHES OF SNOW** FELL ON SPRINGFIELD OVERNIGHT, RESULTING IN BUSINESS AND SCHOOL CLOSURES THROUGHOUT THE CITY. SO THOSE OF YOU LUCKY ENOUGH TO STAY AT HOME TODAY, PULL ON YOUR MITTENS, GET OUT YOUR SLEDS, AND TAKE ADVANTAGE OF THIS **WINTER WONDERLAND!**

UH OH, CHIEF. **"SNOW DAY"**. YOU KNOW WHAT **THAT** MEANS.

YEAH, DON'T EAT THE YELLOW SNOW. I LEARNED MY LESSON THE **LAST** TIME, LOU.

I ♥ N.Y.

NO, I'M TALKING ABOUT ALL THE WEIRD CRIMES THAT HAPPEN ON SNOW DAYS.

IT'S TRUE. SOMETHING ABOUT THE TOWN SHUTTING DOWN BRINGS OUT THE **WEIRDOS** AND THEIR HAIR-BRAINED SCHEMES.

BRRRRING!

AND **SO IT BEGINS,** BOYS...

SPRINGFIELD POLICE. CHIEF WIGGUM SPEAKING.

CHIEF, IT'S LISA SIMPSON! COME QUICK! SOMEONE HAS STOLEN MY POLITICALLY CORRECT **SNOW-PERSON!!**

LET'S ROLL! WE'VE GOT A SNOWMAN THEFT ON EVERGREEN TERRACE!

THAT'S JUST **SICK.**

...AND DON'T FORGET THE SPRINGFIELD SNOWMAN COMPETITION AT TWO O'CLOCK IN THE TOWN SQUARE! THIS YEAR'S GRAND PRIZE IS A BLUE RIBBON AND A COUPON FOR A FREE **COLONOSCOPY** COURTESY OF DR. HIBBERT!

SNOW FALLING ON CHEATERS

WHEERROO!

WHEERROO!

A FEW MINUTES LATER...

TELL ME EXACTLY WHAT HAPPENED, LISA.

AFTER HEARING THAT SCHOOL WAS CLOSED, I STARTED BUILDING MY SNOW-PERSON. I SPENT ABOUT AN HOUR OUTSIDE, THEN WENT IN FOR A COCOA BREAK, BUT WHEN I CAME BACK OUT TO FINISH, IT WAS *GONE!*

ENTER – CRIME SC

ABOUT WHAT TIME WAS THIS?

JUST AFTER MOE PICKED UP MAGGIE AND TOOK HER TO THE PARK TO HELP HER BUILD HER *OWN* SNOWMAN... AROUND NINE A.M.

CHIEF, LOOK AT *THIS!* I FOUND IT NEAR SOME FOOTPRINTS ON THE SIDEWALK.

THEY LEAD FROM THE SIDEWALK TO THE SNOW-PERSON TO THE FRONT DOOR! MEANING THE PERP MUST BE *INSIDE!*

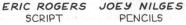

ERIC ROGERS
SCRIPT

JOEY NILGES
PENCILS

MIKE DECARLO
INKS

NATHAN HAMILL
COLORS

KAREN BATES
LETTERS

BILL MORRISON
EDITOR

A MOMENT LATER...

IF IT DON'T *FIT*, YOU MUST *ACQUIT!*

TRUER WORDS WERE NEVER SPOKEN, SIMPSON. WHICH MEANS OUR THIEF MUST BE BART!

NO WAY, MAN! I WAS OUT SLEDDING ALL MORNING! THAT GLOVE MUST'VE DROPPED OUT OF MY POCKET ON MY WAY INSIDE!

WE'LL JUST *SEE* ABOUT THAT. BOYS, CHECK HIS ROOM FOR LISA'S SNOW-PERSON.

IN YOUR *FACE*, BOY!

KNOCK! KNOCK!

OFFICERS, MY BOYS' *SNOW-JESUS* HAS JUST BEEN STOLEN FROM OUR BACKYARD!

WHICH MEANS WE'VE GOT A *PATTERN!*

AND BART *CAN'T* BE THE THIEF 'CAUSE HE WAS IN HERE!

THERE'S NO MORE DEDUCING TO BE DONE HERE! TO THE FLANDERSESESES!

RIGHT HERE IS WHERE THE BOYS WERE BUILDING THEIR VERSION OF THE "LAST SUPPER" FOR THE SNOWMAN COMPETITION. THEY HAD JUST FINISHED JESUS AND CAME TO GET ME, BUT WHEN I CAME OUT, JESUS WAS *GONE!*

MAYBE THAT *SNOW-JUDAS* OVER THERE HAD SOMETHING TO DO WITH IT.

NO, IT WAS *NELSON* AND HIS FRIENDS! JUST BEFORE WE FINISHED JESUS, THEY RODE BY ON THEIR SNOWBOARDS AND MADE FUN OF US!

THEY EVEN SAID THEY'D BE BACK LATER TO PUT THEIR *"FINISHING TOUCH"* ON OUR SNOW-POSTLES!

CHIEF, THESE LOOK LIKE SNOW-BOARD TRACKS. THEY *DEFINITELY* CAME THIS WAY.

THEN LET'S SEE WHERE THEY GO.

AT THE KWIK-E-MART...

...SO YOU'RE SAYING YOU *DIDN'T* TOUCH THE SNOW-JESUS OR LISA'S SNOW-PERSON?

FOR THE LAST TIME, DUDE, WE DIDN'T TAKE ANY STUPID SNOWMEN!

AND IF WE HAD, WHERE WOULD WE *HIDE* THEM?

AND HOW WOULD WE *CARRY THEM* ON OUR SNOWBOARDS?

HEY! IF ANYONE'S GONNA ASK THE *STUPID QUESTIONS* AROUND HERE, IT'S GONNA BE *ME!*

I STILL SAY WE TAKE 'EM IN FOR QUESTIONING, CHIEF.

OFFICERS, I BELIEVE YOU ARE BARKING UP THE *WRONG SKIRT!*

WHY'S THAT?

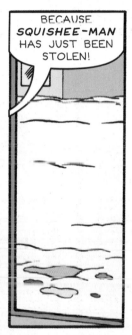

BECAUSE *SQUISHEE-MAN* HAS JUST BEEN STOLEN!

SQUISHEE-MAN?

MY ENTRY INTO THE SNOWMAN COMPETITION! I MADE HIM FROM SNOW AND SQUISHEE. HE'S THE SNOWMAN YOU CAN *EAT* AFTER YOU GROW BORED OF HIS NOTHINGNESS!

SQUISHEE-MAN WAS THERE WHEN WE CAME IN, CHIEF.

WHICH MEANS ONE OF YOUR MOST RECENT CUSTOMERS MUST HAVE TAKEN HIM!

HE MUST HAVE DONE THIS PERPETRATION!

LET'S SHRED!!!

VRROOOMM!

PULL OVER!

GNARLY!

WHEERROO! WHEERROO!

IS THERE, LIKE, SOMETHING TOTALLY WRONG, OFFICER DUDE?

I NEED TO CHECK THIS VEHICLE FOR STOLEN SNOW-MEN, SIR.

NO SNOWMEN HERE, DUDE!

SO THERE ISN'T. BUT I WOULD ADVISE YOU TO WEAR THAT SKI MASK--IT'S *TOO COLD* OUT HERE NOT TO!

FOR *SURE!*

CHIEF, WE JUST GOT A CALL! THERE'S BEEN *ANOTHER* SNOWMAN STOLEN FROM THE *DUFF FACTORY!*

LET'S GO!

DUFFMAN WAS BUILDING TWO PUMPED-UP *DUFF SNOW-GIRLS* FOR THE SNOWMAN COMPETITION! OH YEAH!

BUT WHEN DUFFMAN HAD TO GO INSIDE FOR A TOTALLY AWESOME *POTTY BREAK,* SOMEONE STOLE HIS MASTERPIECE!

ANY IDEA WHO DID IT?

MAYBE IT WAS FAT TONY AND HIS GANG. THEY LEANED ON DUFFMAN AND TOLD HIM THEY PLAN TO MUSCLE IN ON THE BEER BUSINESS WITH THE NEW BREW, "GOOM-BEER."

WE'RE GETTING CLOSER AND CLOSER, BOYS...

TO SOLVING THE CASE, CHIEF?

NO, TO THE *END OF THE DAY* WHEN WE CAN GO HOME. WE MIGHT AS WELL QUESTION FAT TONY AND HIS CREW FIRST.

SOON...

I'M AFRAID YOU MUST HAVE ME CONFUSED WITH SOMEONE WHO IS SOMEWHAT LESS THAN LAW-ABIDING. FOR YOU SEE, I COULD NOT HAVE STOLEN ANY SNOWMEN BECAUSE I WAS AT *THE PIER* ALL MORNING.

DOING WHAT, FAT TONY?

SIMPLY DROPPING OFF A *CARPET ROLL.* JUST ASK THE SEA CAPTAIN.

...*ARRRR,* HE BE TELLING YOU THE TRUTH! I SAW HIM HERE THIS MORNING WITH THAT CARPET.

GEE, CHIEF. LOOKS LIKE WE'VE HIT A DEAD END WITH THIS CASE.

IF'N YE DON'T MIND, I'D BEST BE OFF TO THE TOWN SQUARE. I DON'T WANT TO MISS ANY OF THE *SNOWMAN COMPETITION!*

GOOD NIGHT IN THE MORNING, *THAT'S IT!!*

WHAT'S IT?

THIS SNOWMAN COMPETITION! OUR THIEF IS STEALING SNOWMEN BECAUSE HE OR SHE IS GOING TO *BE THERE* AND HE OR SHE IS MAKING SURE NO ONE HAS A *BETTER SNOWMAN* THAN HE OR SHE DOES!!!

SO HOW ARE WE GONNA CATCH HE OR SHE?

BOYS, WE'RE GOING *DEEP UNDERCOVER* FOR THIS STING! NOW HERE'S THE PLAN...

LATER, IN SPRINGFIELD'S TOWN SQUARE...

WELCOME TO OUR...ER, AH...ANNUAL SNOW-MAN COMPETITION! WE'LL INTRODUCE OUR CONTESTANTS AND PICK A WINNER IN JUST A *FEW SHORT MOMENTS!*

2006 FIRST SNOW SNOWMAN COMPETI!

OH, HEY. WE'RE NOT TOO LATE TO ENTER THE COMPETITION, ARE WE?

YEAH, IT'S JUST A LITTLE SOMETHING WE THREW TOGETHER THIS MORNING...

WE CALL HIM "SNOW CHIEF"!

HEY, I HATE TO BE A BEARER OF STINKY NEWS, BUT I GOTTA CHANGE THE BABY. A LITTLE PRIVACY, HUH?

SURE. WE'LL LEAVE YOU *TOTALLY ALONE*.

JUST DON'T LET ANYTHING HAPPEN TO OUR *SNOWMAN*, OKAY?

SORRY, SNOW-COP, BUT I GOTTA MAKE YOU *DISAPPEAR. NOBODY'S* WINNING THAT BLUE RIBBON EXCEPT *MY LITTLE MAGGIE* HERE!

FREEZE!

WAAH--?!

64

IT'S SOME KINDA *FREAKISH SNOW MONSTER!!*

SLAM!

WHAMM!

OKAY, PAL, YOU'RE UNDER ARRES--

SWEET. DUNKIN'. DONUT.

OH, UMMM... HEH-HEH, WHERE DID ALL THESE SNOWMEN COME FROM?

YOU'RE A REALLY GOOD LISTENER. WANNA GET MARRIED?

LATER

LOOKIT, I'M *REAL SORRY* ABOUT ALL THIS, AND I KNOW I DONE WRONG. I JUST WANTED LITTLE MAGGIE TO WIN. BUT SHE SHOULDN'T SUFFER 'CAUSE OF MY DUMB MISTAKE.

WELL, WHAT DO YOU PROPOSE WE *DO* ABOUT IT?

A LITTLE LATER, IN THE MIDDLE OF TOWN...

WELL THEN, WITHOUT ANY FURTHER DELAY, LET'S SEE OUR SNOWMEN!!

THIS IS THE *ONLY* ONE??

:SIGH: I GUESS HE'S THE WINNER THEN.

WAIT!!

I CALL IT, "CRAZY, SEXY, COOL: A SELF-PORTRAIT".

I BRAKE *for* TAUNTAUNS

THIS IS MAGGIE'S ENTRY!

NOW *THAT'S* A SNOWMAN!

THE WINNER... ER, AH...IS *MAGGIE SIMPSON!*

WORST. LAST-MINUTE ENTRY. *EVER!*

I JUST *KNEW* SHE'D WIN!

AT LAST, CECIL, WE'VE FINALLY DUG OUR WAY OUT OF *PRISON!* AND JUST LOOK--UNATTENDED SNOWMOBILES FOR *OUR GETAWAY!*

HOW *FORTUITOUS!*

UH-OH. *THIS* AIN'T GOOD...

THE END